# EXTREME
# RAINFOREST

WELDON OWEN INC.
CEO, President  Terry Newell
VP, Sales and New Business Development  Amy Kaneko

VP, Publisher  Roger Shaw
Executive Editor  Mariah Bear
Editor  Lucie Parker
Project Editors  Nam Nguyen, Sarah Hines Stephens
Editorial Assistant  Emelie Griffin

Creative Director  Kelly Booth
Senior Designer  William Mack
Assistant Designer  Michel Gadwa

Production Director  Chris Hemesath
Production Manager  Michelle Duggan
Color Manager  Teri Bell

Library of Congress Cataloging-in-Publication
information is on file with the Publisher.

ISBN: 978-0-545-34739-6

This edition published by Scholastic Inc.,
557 Broadway, New York, NY 10012
by arrangement with Weldon Owen Inc.

Distributed in Canada by Scholastic Canada Ltd., Markham, Ontario
Distributed in the UK by Scholastic UK, Coventry, Warwickshire
Distributed in New Zealand by Scholastic New Zealand Ltd., Greenmount, Auckland

A Weldon Owen Production
415 Jackson Street
San Francisco, California 94111

Printed in Shenzhen, China, by Asia Pacific Offset.
10 9 8 7 6 5 4 3 2 1
2011  2012  2013  2014  2015  2016  2017  2018  2019  2020

# EXTREME
# RAINFOREST

# CONTENTS

## MEET THE BEASTS

Rainforests cover only six percent of Earth's surface, yet they support more than half of the world's plant and animal species. In this wet and often unstable environment, how do the sneaky creatures creeping on the forest floor, the amazing animals lurking in plant pools, and the large beasts navigating the treacherous treetops adapt for survival? Toxic skin, poison-injecting fangs, sonic muscles, and hidden wings are just a few of the astounding tools that rainforest animals have at their disposal. Even so, thriving on the leafy forest floor or in the branches of this high-rise habitat is no picnic. Step into the rainforest and see for yourself.

# MIRACLE WALKER

Brilliant green and equipped with flashing tails, sharp claws, and plumelike crests of skin crowning their heads, basilisk lizards stand out in the rainforest crowd. These dazzling reptiles also have a skill that no other animals of their size possess: when pursued, they can run on water, leaving enemies in their dust—or rather, their spray.

**GEOGRAPHY**
Southern Mexico through Central America to Ecuador

**HABITAT**
Streaks past dense vegetation, shrubs, and trees near water

## GREEN BASILISK LIZARD
*Basiliscus plumifrons*

LENGTH: **2.5 FEET (75 CM)**   WEIGHT: **3 OUNCES (85 G)**

**INTELLIGENCE**
■■■■■■□□□□

**AGILITY**
■■■■■■■■■□

**STRENGTH**
■■■□□□□□□□

**ENDURANCE**
■■■■■□□□□□

**SPEED**
■■□□□□□□□□

**EVASION**
■■■■■■■■□□

**PREY**

**GRASSHOPPERS**
Basilisk lizards hunt near the base of trees and on the ground, looking to snare juicy grasshoppers.

**ENEMY**

**HEADING FOR DANGER**
When hanging out on the forest floor, away from watery escape routes, basilisk lizards risk being hunted by snakes. These slithery predators often swallow lizards headfirst to avoid getting scratched.

**FLYING FLAGS**
The male's bright, fanning head crest attracts females looking for a mate.

**BALANCE BEAM**
The lizard's tail makes up 18 percent of its weight, providing counterbalance and keeping the lizard upright while running.

**SUPERPOWER**
Water walking
**EQUIPMENT**
Long, thin tail; sharp, climbing claws; wide, slapping feet
**WEAKNESS**
Large size (big basilisks are too slow to run far over water)
**FACT**
Basilisks can swim well in water when they get tired of running across it.

**HANGING HOOKS**
Sharp claws on each foot grip tightly to tree branches, aiding in climbing.

**COOL TREADS**
Long, spread-out toes create enough force to propel lizards across water at speeds of up to 7 miles per hour (11 kph).

## SUPERPOWERS
Crushing jaws; extreme agility

## EQUIPMENT
Powerful legs; large paws

## WEAKNESS
Extreme self-confidence (jaguars often walk out in the open, making themselves easy targets)

## FACT
Most jaguars are yellow with black spots, but the black jaguar's skin contains more melanin, which makes it darker.

## HEADLIGHTS
A reflective layer in the back of the eye doubles the available light, boosting the jaguar's vision in dim conditions.

## MIGHTY COMPACTOR
Large, dense jaws kill by crushing the skulls or shattering the necks of prey with a single bite.

## CRUISING ZONE
Jaguars patrol a territory of up to 60 square miles (155 sq km). Male cats refuse to share turf with other males.

## CAN OPENERS
Thirty sharp teeth are the perfect tools for breaking turtle shells, gnawing holes in scaled caimans, and prying apart prey.

## GEOGRAPHY

Mexico through Central America to northern Argentina

## HABITAT

Patrols tropical forests, deciduous forests, savannas, and scrublands

# DARK STALKER

Black jaguars eat anything that moves, from snails to deer. These densely built predators have thick legs, large feet, and strong jaws, perfectly suited to their powerful attacks. At home in the trees or swimming the flooded rainforest, jaguars are extremely intelligent: they're the only big cats clever enough to tackle prey as well-armored as turtles and caimans.

**ENEMY**

### POACHERS

Poachers kill jaguars as well as many of their food sources. There may be as few as 15,000 or so of these beautiful cats left in the wild.

**PREY**

### CAPYBARAS

Jaguars are big cats, so it makes sense that they like to eat large rodents. Capybaras weigh as much as 140 pounds (65 kg).

### TAPIRS

Jaguars don't hesitate to pounce on prey much larger than themselves, like tapirs, which measure up to 8 feet (2.5 m) long.

### CAIMANS

Jaguars hunt caimans and crack their tough armor by chewing through the caimans' sides, where there are no protective scales.

## BLACK JAGUAR
*Panthera onca*

LENGTH: **5 FEET (1.5 M)**   WEIGHT: **150 POUNDS (70 KG)**

**INTELLIGENCE**
■■■■■■■■■□□

**AGILITY**
■■■■■■■■■■□□

**STRENGTH**
■■■■■■■■□□□

**ENDURANCE**
■■■■■■■■■□□

**SPEED**
■■■■■■■■□□

**ATTACK**
■■■■■■■■■□□

# SUPER GENIUS

The brainiacs of the bird world, African gray parrots are famous for their smarts and astounding speaking ability. Sadly, since they only live in a small area of central and west Africa, and their intelligence makes them such attractive pets, they have become endangered by the people who illegally trap and sell them. Left in the wild, African grays learn their own language from their parents and live together in highly social groups.

## GEOGRAPHY
West and central Africa

## HABITAT
Flocks in canopies of lowland rainforests

## AFRICAN GRAY PARROT
*Psittacus erithacus*

LENGTH: **13 INCHES (33 CM)**   WEIGHT: **1 POUND (0.45 KG)**

| INTELLIGENCE | AGILITY |
|---|---|
| ■■■■■■■■■■ | ■■■■■■■■■□ |

| STRENGTH | ENDURANCE |
|---|---|
| ■■■■■□□□□□ | ■■■■□□□□□□ |

| SPEED | EVASION |
|---|---|
| ■■□□□□□□ | ■■■■■□□□□□ |

**ENEMY**

### PALM NUT VULTURES
These vultures have a favorite food in common with African grays—palm nut seeds. The bullies are often seen harassing parrot flocks in treetops.

**TOOL TIME**

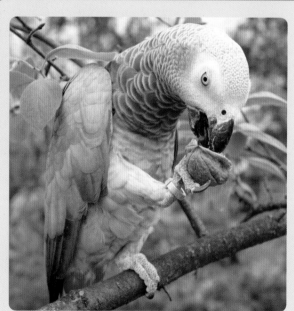

### BEAK BREAKER
African gray parrots use their sharp, ever-growing beaks and muscular, fingerlike tongues to position and crack nuts. Their beaks can grow strong enough to cut through wire fencing!

**RAIN SLICKER**
Preen glands secrete natural oils that parrots spread on their feathers to keep them supple and waterproof.

**CAGE JAW**
This parrot's upper jaw is reinforced with multiple strips of bone. These extra bone segments add strength and protect against impact.

**SUPERPOWERS**
Masterful mimicry; superior intelligence

**EQUIPMENT**
Powerful beak; flexible jaw

**WEAKNESS**
Takes 60 to 70 days for babies to leave the nest

**FACT**
Lacking vocal chords, African grays make sound by blowing across the tops of their airways.

**HOOK MOUTH**
A superelastic ligament attaches a parrot's upper beak and skull. The extra flexibility allows the bird to hook and slide along branches with its mouth.

**SUPERPOWER**
Extreme energy efficiency

**EQUIPMENT**
Three sharp claws; extra neck vertebrae; absorbent fur

**WEAKNESS**
Poor temperature control (dependent on warm environment)

**FACT**
Although awkward on land, sloths are excellent swimmers.

**HANDY CLAWS**
Three long claws on each leg are used for fighting off predators and hanging from tree limbs.

**ABOUT-FACE**
Sloths have extra neckbones, allowing them to turn their heads 270 degrees.

**GREEN ENERGY**
Sloth fur absorbs water and encourages the growth of algae, which provides both camouflage and nutrients.

**COMB-OVER**
Since sloths hang belly-up, their hair parts along their stomachs to direct rainwater off their bodies.

## GEOGRAPHY
From south Central America to northern Argentina

## HABITAT
Naps in mid- to upper-forest canopies

## SLOW AND STEADY
Despite their reputation, sloths aren't lazy—they're just energy efficient. Their low metabolism and creeping pace make them well suited for life as large vegetarian mammals. By moving at an average speed of 1,000 feet per hour (300 meters per hour) and often sleeping 20 out of 24 hours, they expend fewer than 100 calories a day—less energy than is found in a slice of bread.

**ENEMY**

### JAGUARS
Sloths are vulnerable to jaguar attacks on the ground, so they only descend from the trees to go to the bathroom every three to four days.

**IN ACTION**

### COMMANDO CRAWL
Long, curved claws are great for hanging in trees but terrible for walking on land. To move on the ground, sloths crawl slowly and awkwardly—pulling themselves forward with their claws.

## THREE-TOED SLOTH
*Bradypus tridactylus*

LENGTH: **2 FEET (60 CM)** WEIGHT: **11 POUNDS (5 KG)**

INTELLIGENCE
■■■■■■□□□□

AGILITY
■■■■■□□□□□

STRENGTH
■■□□□□□□□□

ENDURANCE
■■■■□□□□□□

SPEED
■□□□□□□□□□

EVASION
■■□□□□□□□□

## NORTH AMERICA

The temperate, mossy rainforest of North America's Pacific Northwest boasts the coldest rainforest climate and the most ancient trees, along with landslides and avalanches.

## WESTERN AFRICA

Once an unbroken expanse, Africa's rainforests are now solitary pockets on misty mountain islands. These islands receive less than two hours of sunlight during the rainy season.

## SOUTH AMERICA

South America's rainforests cover nearly half the continent. They are the world's most diverse in spite of seasonal rains that flood forests up to 25 feet (7.5 m).

# RAINFORESTS OF THE WORLD

An average annual rainfall of 8 to 15 feet (2.5–4.5 m) is what makes a rainforest a rainforest. Although they share other common traits, including dense tree canopies and amazing biodiversity (the variety of animals and plants they host), differences in climate and geography make each of the world's rainforests as unique as their plant and animal populations. Here are the Earth's rainforests and some of the creatures that call them home.

### ROOSEVELT ELKS
**NORTH AMERICA**

The slick, woody terrain of the temperate rainforests requires sure footing and a stomach for bark. The well-adapted Roosevelt elk, also known as the Olympic elk, enjoys both.

### MARMOSETS
**SOUTH AMERICA**

A marmoset's long tail and opposable thumbs help them negotiate the dense Amazon forest's canopy. Specialized teeth allow them to gnaw the gum out of tree trunks.

### FLYING SQUIRRELS
#### ASIA

When navigating trees of various heights, flying squirrels' wings give them the advantage of moving from high to low canopies with speed and ease—crucial when they're being pursued by larger and faster predators.

### TREE KANGAROOS
#### OCEANIA

Oceania's rainforests are home to many marsupials, like the tree kangaroo. This kangaroo is at ease on the ground or in the forest canopies. It uses its massive hind limbs and long tail to shimmy up and down tree trunks.

### GORILLAS
#### WESTERN AFRICA

African rainforests are home to many large mammals. Gorillas survive on the continent's misty slopes by filling their big bellies with huge quantities of plants.

### FOSSAS
#### MADAGASCAR

Fossas live only in Madagascar, where they enjoy life unchallenged by Africa's fierce predators. A relative of the mongoose, the fossa grows up to 6 feet (2 m) long and has retractable claws and a long, balancing tail.

### ASIA

Asia is home to one-fourth of the world's rainforests. This dramatic region is subject to typhoons, monsoons, earthquakes, and, during periods of drought, even fires.

### OCEANIA

Clusters of trees, rather than unbroken forest, characterize the dense rainforests that grow along Australia's western coast and across all of New Guinea.

### MADAGASCAR

Madagascar's rainforests have developed in isolation from Africa for millions of years. Ninety percent of the island's plants and shrubs are found nowhere else on Earth.

# KING OF THE HILL

Tamanduas, also known as lesser anteaters, may be smaller than their oversize cousins, but they are better adapted to living in rainforests. Unlike ground-dwelling giant anteaters, tamanduas can prowl both on the forest floor and in the trees, and they hunt after dark. They use their sharp sense of smell to track down meals at night, when termites are most active.

## GEOGRAPHY
Venezuela to northern Argentina and Uruguay

## HABITAT
Climbs among branches near water in rainforests and savannas

## TAMANDUA
*Tamandua tetradactyla*

LENGTH: **3 FEET (1 M)**   WEIGHT: **11 POUNDS (5 KG)**

INTELLIGENCE
■■■■■■□■■■□

AGILITY
■■■■■■■□■■□

STRENGTH
■■■□■■■■■■■

ENDURANCE
■■■□■■■■■■■

SPEED
■■■■■□■■■■□

EVASION
■■■■■□■■■■□

PREY

### TERMITES
Tamanduas are related to anteaters. They eat only ants and termites, preferring varieties that make their nests in the branches of trees.

TOOL TIME

### FIGHTING STANCE
When threatened, tamanduas brandish their sharp claws like blades and use their tails as tripods to stand upright. In trees they hang by their tails—keeping their arms free for slashing.

**CHEMICAL CLOUD**
If threatened, tamanduas release a stench from glands below their tails that deters predators.

**NOSE KNOWS**
Supersensitive noses expertly sniff out ant and termite nests.

**SUPERPOWER**
Specialized night hunting

**EQUIPMENT**
Clawed feet; prehensile tail; long snout and tongue

**WEAKNESS**
Awkward walkers (must walk on heels due to long claws)

**FACT**
Tamanduas sweat only through their noses, lips, and toes.

**SAFETY HARNESS**
A tamandua's grasping, prehensile tail is as long as its body and wraps around branches to hold them aloft while they hunt.

**LINT ROLLER**
The tamandua's tongue can grow up to 16 inches (40 cm) long. It is equipped with tiny spikes that snare termites.

**INFRARED WEB**
Heat-sensing pits are set at different angles to cast a wide sensory net—perfect for locating prey.

**SUPERPOWERS**
Camouflage; heat detection

**EQUIPMENT**
Infrared detectors; curved teeth; muscular body; prehensile tail

**WEAKNESS**
Weak eyesight (boas depend on scent and heat to track prey)

**FACT**
Emerald tree boas are born reddish-brown and turn green as they grow older.

**MEAT HOOKS**
Large front teeth are curved backward to embed deeper into struggling prey.

**WHIP GRIP**
Boas hang suspended from branches by their prehensile tails. They use their coils like ropes to descend on unwitting animals.

### GEOGRAPHY
Venezuela to northern Bolivia and northern Brazil

### HABITAT
Slithers in forest canopies, swamps, and rivers

## THE BIG SQUEEZE
Emerald tree boas are beautiful by day, curled in the rainforest canopy. But by night, stealthily traveling through the treetops looking for dinner, they are decidedly deadly. Once boas locate their prey, they wrap it up in their long, muscular bodies and squeeze tighter and tighter, eventually killing the animal before eating it headfirst and whole.

### PREY

**TURNIP-TAILED GECKOS**
Emerald boas kill lizards such as turnip-tailed geckos by constriction. Once the lizard stops breathing, the snake swallows it whole.

### TOOL TIME

**UP A TREE**
Bright green boa scales are scattered with white markings. When boas lie coiled over branches in the rainforest canopy, their bodies look like leaves dappled with sunlight.

## EMERALD TREE BOA
*Corallus caninus*

LENGTH: **6 FEET (2 M)**   DIAMETER: **2 INCHES (5 CM)**

**INTELLIGENCE**
■■■■■■□□□□

**AGILITY**
■■■■■■■□□□

**STRENGTH**
■■■■■□■■■■■

**ENDURANCE**
■■■■■□■■■■

**SPEED**
■■■□■■■

**ATTACK**
■■■■■■■■■■

# MULTILEGGED MONSTER

Giant centipedes are the ultimate all-terrain terror. Their long, segmented bodies are lined with dozens of gripping legs, allowing them to stalk their next meal as easily from the ground as they can hanging from the ceiling of a cave. Once they sense their prey, centipedes attack with powerful fangs, injecting victims with lethal poison that stuns first, then kills.

**GEOGRAPHY**
Colombia, Venezuela, the Guianas, western Brazil

**HABITAT**
Creeps through soil, leaf litter, and rotten wood

## GIANT CENTIPEDE
*Scolopendra gigantea*

LENGTH: **10 INCHES (25 CM)**  WEIGHT: **0.5 OUNCES (14 G)**

| INTELLIGENCE | AGILITY |
| --- | --- |
| ■■■■■□□□□□ | ■■■■■■□□□□ |

| STRENGTH | ENDURANCE |
| --- | --- |
| ■■■■□□□□□□ | ■■■■■■□□□□ |

| SPEED | ATTACK |
| --- | --- |
| ■■■■■■□□□□ | ■■■■■■□□□□ |

### TOOL TIME

**CENTIPEDE POISON**
The centipede's two black-tipped fangs inject poison into its prey. This poison slows prey, while the centipede wraps its many legs around it.

### PREY

**MICE**
Mice and centipedes both live on the forest floor. If their paths cross, a mouse will likely get a lethal hug from its neighbor.

**TOADS**
Centipedes attack prey, such as toads, by biting the toad's neck to stun it. Then the centipede eats the toad down to its chest and belly.

**BATS**
Using their rear legs to cling to cave roofs, centipedes dangle head-down in the dark to snare bats out of the air with their front feet.

**BIG-HEARTED**
Extremely long hearts run the length of giant centipedes' bodies.

**SHARP TURNS**
Segmented bodies bend to slip through crevices and coil around prey.

**SUPERPOWERS**
Flexibility; multilegged gripping action; deadly poison

**EQUIPMENT**
Segmented body; poisonous fangs; sensitive antennae

**WEAKNESS**
Dries up without humidity

**FACT**
Centipede poison paralyzes prey so that it becomes numb to sensory information.

**AUTOMATIC INJECTION**
Pinchers inject pressure-released poison into anything caught in a centipede's clutches.

**DARK SCOPE**
Centipedes' antennae sense vibrations and enable them to locate their prey in pitch darkness.

## ELEVATOR EYES
Poison frogs blink by lowering their bulging eyes into their sockets. The pressure also helps them swallow.

## WARNING SIGN
Vivid coloring lets predators know these frogs are poisonous—stay away!

## SUPERPOWER
Toxic touch

## EQUIPMENT
Long fingers; jumping legs; bright warning coloration

## WEAKNESS
Thin skin that dehydrates quickly

## FACT
Poison frog fathers pee on egg nests to keep their babies moist until they hatch.

## SNACK TIME
Mother frogs feed unfertilized eggs to their tadpoles, laying eggs in the tadpole's pool for easy access.

## SLIME SHIELD
This frog's slime layer helps it absorb water from the air and protect it from water loss.

### GEOGRAPHY

Nicaragua, Panama, Costa Rica

### HABITAT

Hops around in forest-floor leaf litter, on trees, and in bromeliads

## COLORFUL CHEMIST

Small poison frogs (also called poison arrow frogs) hunt in broad daylight, fearlessly flashing their bright colors before would-be predators. Why so bold? These tiny amphibians produce one of the world's deadliest poisons. Any snake foolish enough to eat a poison frog will spit it out, then writhe or fall into a coma (sometimes for hours) before recovering from a single tiny taste.

**ALLY**

### BROMELIADS

Rainforest bromeliads have cup-shaped leaves that hold water. They provide protected pools for developing tadpoles.

## STRAWBERRY POISON FROG
### *Dendrobates pumilio*

LENGTH: **1 INCH (2.5 CM)**  WEIGHT: **0.02 OUNCES (0.5 G)**

**LIFE OR DEATH**

### FOOD POISONING

To gather ingredients for the deadly mix they wear on their skin, poison frogs eat poisonous beetles, mites, and ants. Once ingested, frogs chemically change these poisons, making them deadlier.

**INTELLIGENCE**

**AGILITY**

**STRENGTH**

**ENDURANCE**

**SPEED**

**DEFENSE**

# SWARMING SCISSORS

Red-bellied piranhas have such fearsome reputations as people-eaters that locals wrap their legs with cloth for protection before walking in piranha-infested pools. Though these omnivores have been known to scavenge sizable dead or dying mammals, piranhas only attack large healthy prey when food is scarce. They gather in schools of ten to 100—more for protection than attack.

## RED-BELLIED PIRANHA
*Pygocentrus nattereri*

LENGTH: **5 INCHES (13 CM)**   WEIGHT: **2.5 POUNDS (1 KG)**

**INTELLIGENCE**
■■■■■■□□□□□

**AGILITY**
■■■■■■■■■□□

**STRENGTH**
■■■□■■■■■■□

**ENDURANCE**
■■■■■■□■■■□

**SPEED**
■■■■□■■□□□□

**EVASION**
■■■■■■■■■■□

### ENEMIES

**BOTOS**
Amazon river dolphins are adept at navigating flooded forests and shrinking pools, where piranha schools are often trapped.

**CAIMANS**
These many-toothed alligators have tough skin and no fear of sharp piranha teeth. They readily seek out piranha snacks.

### IN ACTION

**FEEDING FRENZY**
Red-bellied piranha schools are the industrial-strength vacuums of rainforest rivers. They suck up other fish, leaves, fruit, seeds, insects, and dead animals.

## BUILT-IN AMP

Piranhas create sound by contracting muscles next to their air bladders. The bladders amplify noise, making it easier for other fish to hear.

### SUPERPOWER
Group attack and defense

### EQUIPMENT
Flat body; sharp interlocking teeth; sonic muscles

### WEAKNESS
Inflexible eyes (piranhas are nearsighted)

### FACT
Smaller piranhas attack more aggressively than larger ones.

## SHEAR GENIUS

Razor-sharp teeth cut out bits of meat, like scissors. Piranhas stay sharp by growing replacement teeth every four months.

## SIXTH SENSE

Muscles along a piranha's sides sense vibrations from changing currents and other fish.

## PERFECT FIT

Cusps on each tooth fit together when the jaws are closed. They keep food from floating away.

## SPEEDY BYPASS

Since blood is already liquid, it can be digested quickly, providing vampire bats with almost instant energy.

## HEAT DETECTION

Heat-seeking noses help bats on the hunt by sensing blood vessels near the surface of prey's skin.

## SUPERPOWERS

Superleaping ability; chemically enhanced saliva

## EQUIPMENT

Heat-sensitive nose; grooved, lapping tongue

## WEAKNESS

Will die within three days without food

## FACT

To avoid becoming too heavy to fly after large meals, bats often urinate while eating.

## SIPHON SUCTION

Bats don't suck blood—they lap it up. Two grooves on their tongues help keep the blood flowing into their mouths.

## GYMNASTIC ACTION

Strong upper bodies let bats leap, cartwheel, or jerk sideways to avoid being squashed by large prey.

## GEOGRAPHY

Mexico through the western coast of South America

## HABITAT

Hangs out in caves, tree hollows, and abandoned buildings

# BLOOD WRAITH

The stuff of legend, tiny vampire bats are versatile, fierce, and opportunistic. They are the only animals able to leap vertically into flight, and they're one of three bat species that eat blood exclusively. Feared for spreading rabies, yet valued for chemicals in their saliva, vampire bats have earned their creepy reputation by stealthily lapping the blood of their prey.

### TOOL TIME

### DSPA

Bat saliva contains draculin, which keeps blood from clotting. Doctors use DSPA derived from bat saliva to prevent brain clots.

### PREY

### COWS

Vampire bats prefer their beef rare. They sneak up on cows at night and drain fresh blood, while the cows sleep.

### CHICKENS

After painlessly slicing a chicken's foot, a bat will feed on the trickle of blood. Repeat visits can weaken and kill the bird.

### RODENTS

Before humans introduced cows into rainforest areas, bats got the majority of their mammal blood from rodents.

## COMMON VAMPIRE BAT
### *Desmodus rotunda*

LENGTH: **3 INCHES (7.5 CM)**   WEIGHT: **1 OUNCE (30 G)**

| INTELLIGENCE | AGILITY |
|---|---|
| STRENGTH | ENDURANCE |
| SPEED | DEFENSE |

# DRESSED TO KILL

Despite its size, the tiger is nearly invisible in the forests it stalks, as its light and dark stripes break up the shape of its body and help it blend into undergrowth. These hungry hunters are the largest cats in the world and won't hesitate to attack, whether in defense of their territory or for food. In one year, a single tiger may eat 50 to 60 large animals—that's 4 tons (3.5 tonnes) of meat!

**GEOGRAPHY**
India, China, Russia, Southeast Asia, Indonesia

**HABITAT**
Stalks through tropical and dry forests, grasslands, and mangroves

## TIGER
*Panthera tigris*

LENGTH: **9 FEET (2.75 M)**    WEIGHT: **400 POUNDS (180 KG)**

**INTELLIGENCE**
■■■■■■■□□□

**AGILITY**
■■■■■■■□□□

**STRENGTH**
■■■■■■■■■

**ENDURANCE**
■■■■■■■■□

**SPEED**
■■■■■■□□□

**ATTACK**
■■■■■■■■□

### ENEMY

**DHOLES**
Though they are much smaller, dholes hunt within tiger ranges and compete for prey. To keep a tiger at bay, dholes attack as a pack.

### PREY

**RHINOS**
Tigers are at the top of the food chain and large enough to risk hunting supersize food sources, like rhinoceros calves.

**WATER BUFFALO**
Webbed feet make tigers excellent swimmers and give them the advantage when hunting slow water buffalo.

**ASIAN WILD PIGS**
Wild pigs travel in groups through rainforests, making these easily available porkers a staple meal.

**ULTRASOUND**
Large, swiveling ears hear sounds five to ten times higher in pitch than humans can hear.

**DEADLY DAGGERS**
A tiger's canines can grow up to 3 inches (7.5 cm) in length. Gaps in the back allow teeth to sink deeper into flesh.

**QUANTUM LEAP**
Strong hind legs can propel a tiger through the air 26 feet (8 m) in a single pounce.

**SURE FOOTING**
Long hairs along a tiger's ankles sense surroundings and help him walk silently, without looking.

**SUPERPOWER**
Peerless patience (tigers can stalk prey for more than an hour)

**EQUIPMENT**
Sharp claws; long canine teeth; webbed paws; sensitive ears

**WEAKNESS**
Slow over long distances

**FACT**
Tigers can swim fully submerged to attack prey from underneath.

## HIDE AND SEEK

The jungles of the rainforest house a lot of hungry mouths—all of them on the verge of eating or being eaten. In this wild free-for-all, species with strategies for remaining undetected have the best chance of surviving. Camouflage (looking like the natural surroundings) and mimicry (resembling a more dangerous animal or a part of another animal) are effective survival strategies.

### EVIL TWIN

Imitation is the highest form of flattery—and a clever strategy for survival, too. Mimicking the traits of a more dangerous animal keeps many less harmful critters from being eaten. For example, nonpoisonous sanguine mimic frogs (bottom) closely resemble the toxic Ecuadorian poison frog (top).

## HEADS OR TAILS

Many moth- and butterfly-wing patterns use mimicry to confuse both predators and prey. Often, these wing patterns look like teeth or giant eyes. The Goliath moth is the largest moth in the world, and it appears to have a big bird beak on each of its wings to keep it safe.

## FLASH OF BRILLIANCE

Fooling the eye isn't just about blending in—another effective form of camouflage is all about dazzling. Bright, bold coloration protects flocks of lorikeets by confusing would-be predators and making it difficult for them to single out a single victim.

## BARKING UP THE WRONG TREE

Asia's Omei tree frog is not only colored like tree bark, it also has bumpy skin that resembles the bark's rough texture.

**SPIDER SENSE**
The many hairs along this spider's legs and body detect the movement of other creatures.

**POP TOP**
Spiders molt as they grow. After opening a hole in their exoskeleton, they crawl out from inside their old shell.

**SUPERPOWERS**
Large size; pouncing attack

**EQUIPMENT**
Eight strong legs; irritating hairs; poison-filled fangs

**WEAKNESS**
Bad eyesight (can only see a short distance in front of it)

**FACT**
Tarantulas can slowly regrow missing legs.

**HOLLOW BLADES**
Red venom-filled fangs inject poison that digests the spider's prey before it's eaten.

**HAIR SPRAY**
When provoked, these spiders fling stinging hairs that irritate their pursuers' eyes and skin.

## GEOGRAPHY
Eastern Brazil

## HABITAT
Creeps over rainforest floors

# PINK MONSTER

Brazilian salmon pink tarantulas get their name from the rosy-tipped hairs that cover their bodies. One of the largest spiders in the world, these tarantulas fearlessly roam the forest floor looking for prey and aggressively attack anything they perceive as a threat. If they happen upon a nest, these bird eaters will gladly dine on the chicks of ground-dwelling birds.

## PREY

### FROGS
Brazilian salmon pinks don't eat birds often. They more commonly make meals of frogs, snakes, and insects.

## BRAZILIAN SALMON PINK
*Lasiodora parahybana*

LEG SPAN: **10 INCHES (25 CM)**

## ENEMY

### STUNNING STINGERS
Brazilian salmon pinks are defenseless against small spider wasps. After paralyzing the spider with a sting, a wasp lays its eggs inside the spider's body. Once hatched, wasp larvae eat their way out.

| INTELLIGENCE | AGILITY |
|---|---|
| STRENGTH | ENDURANCE |
| SPEED | ATTACK |

# BREATH TAKER

Green anacondas are the world's largest and most aquatic constrictors. With reported lengths of 38 feet (11.5 m) and top weights of 550 pounds (250 kg), it's no surprise that this snake's giant size has terrified many, so much so that its Tamil name translates to "elephant killer." These snakes don't kill elephants, but they do swallow prey whole up to 6 feet (2 m) in length. That's bigger than the average adult man.

## GEOGRAPHY
The Guianas; Orinoco and Amazon river basins

## HABITAT
Squeezes through swamps, marshlands, and slow rivers

## GREEN ANACONDA
*Eunectes murinus*

LENGTH: **20 FEET (6 M)**   WEIGHT: **330 POUNDS (150 KG)**

INTELLIGENCE
■■■■■■■■■■■

AGILITY
■■■■■■■■■■■

STRENGTH
■■■■■■■■■■■

ENDURANCE
■■■■■■■■■■■

SPEED
■■■■■■■■■■■

ATTACK
■■■■■■■■■■■

## PREY

### MARSH DEER
The average green anaconda is 20 feet (6 m) in length and has no problem swallowing marsh deer that measure 6 feet (2 m).

### SHARP-SPINED CATFISH
Anacondas spend most of their time in the water, so it's no surprise that they like to eat large river animals, such as sharp-spined catfish.

### PECCARIES
Anacondas snare peccaries with a single bite. The snakes then wrap around their piglike prey, tightening their coils each time the peccaries exhale.

### CAIMANS
In river battles that pit a caiman's snapping jaws against an anaconda's constricting coils, huge anacondas usually come out on top.

**FLOTATION DEVICE**
Naturally buoyant, anacondas swim the same way they move on land—by wriggling their long bodies.

**STINK SHIELD**
Anacondas produce an odor that prevents ticks and mites from feeding on them.

**CONTACT LENS**
Clear scales, called brille, cover an anaconda's eyes to tightly seal out both air and water.

**SNORKEL TUBE**
Windpipes extend to the front of the mouth, allowing snakes to breathe while they swallow meals whole, which can take hours.

**SUPERPOWERS**
Supersize; supreme swimming

**EQUIPMENT**
Six rows of hooking teeth; elastic jaws; strong, squeezing coils

**WEAKNESS**
Overheats easily in the dry season

**FACT**
Anacondas "hear" by sensing vibrations around them with their jawbones.

### SUPERPOWER
Daredevil leaps and glides

### EQUIPMENT
Tiny claws; gliding membrane; long bushy tail

### WEAKNESS
Cold intolerance (sugar gliders must hibernate on cold days)

### FACT
Marsupial gliders carry young in pouches that protect their babies from the impact of landing.

### STEERING RODS
Gliders steer like superheroes by dipping their arms to go left or right or even to make U-turns.

### HAIR-RAISING
Each strand of fur helps increase lift, keeping the marsupial airborne longer.

### STRAIGHT SHOOTER
Bushy glider tails work like rudders to create drag and keep flyers facing forward.

### THUMBS-UP
Gliders' wing tips are connected to their thumbs. Pointing their thumbs up angles their skin flaps for smooth sailing.

## GEOGRAPHY
New Guinea; northern and eastern Australia

## HABITAT
Glides through rainforest midstories

# HIGH FLYER

It takes a lot of time to climb up and down trees, especially if you live in the high-rise canopy of the rainforest. Sugar gliders cut down on their commute by vaulting from tree to tree. Special skin flaps beneath their arms extend like wings to increase hang time and keep these gliders airborne for as far as 135 feet (40 m) per flight.

**PREY**

### PAPUAN WEEVILS
Sugar gliders live off sap and nectar but often add crunch to their diet by munching on insects, such as Papuan weevils.

**TOOL TIME**

### WONDER WING
A sugar glider's patagium (the skin connected to the arm) extends to create a thin "wing" perfect for gliding. When not in use, the flap of skin folds up neatly so it doesn't get caught on branches.

## SUGAR GLIDER
*Petaurus breviceps*

LENGTH: **15 INCHES (40 CM)**   WEIGHT: **4 OUNCES (115 G)**

INTELLIGENCE

AGILITY

STRENGTH

ENDURANCE

SPEED

EVASION

# TALONS OF TERROR

The largest eagle in the world is no gentle giant. With talons up to 5 inches (13 cm) long, ankles thicker than a child's wrist, and a wingspan measuring up to 7 feet (2.25 m), this king of the sky can capture animals as large as itself. While holding its victim aloft, a harpy eagle will deliver a killing stab to the heart of its prey using specialized piercing talons.

### GEOGRAPHY
Southeastern Mexico, across Amazon river basin, to southern Brazil

### HABITAT
Swoops in tropical forest canopies and understories

## HARPY EAGLE
*Harpia harpyja*

LENGTH: **3 FEET (1 M)**   WEIGHT: **16 POUNDS (7.25 KG)**

INTELLIGENCE
■■■■■■■□■■□

AGILITY
■■■■■■■■■□□

STRENGTH
■■■■■■■■□□

ENDURANCE
■■■■■■□□□□

SPEED
■■■■■■■□□□

EVASION
■■■■■□□□□□

**PREY**

### HOWLER MONKEYS
Investigations of debris beneath harpy eagles' nests have revealed howler monkey bones— evidence of many monkey meals.

**LIFE AND DEATH**

### AMBUSH HUNTERS
Harpy eagles prefer to sit perfectly still in trees until they spot their victims. Once they have sighted their prey, the eagles drop down and give chase through the trees with claws extended.

**FARSIGHTED**
Harpy eagles can spot a small mouse from 660 feet (200 m) away.

**PRECISION PIERCING**
The death blow of a harpy eagle leaves a puncture wound in the victim's chest that measures 0.5 inches (13 mm).

**CRUSHER BLADES**
Harpy eagles can exert enough pressure with their claws to smash bones and instantly kill prey.

**SUPERPOWERS**
Extreme vision; piercing talons

**EQUIPMENT**
Head crest; steering tail; massive claws

**WEAKNESS**
Fixed eyes (must move head to look in other directions)

**FACT**
Harpies reach gliding speeds of up to 50 miles per hour (80 kph).

**REAR SPOILER**
The short, broad tail makes it easy for this bird to weave through dense treetops.

## SUPERPOWERS
Flexibility; echolocation (using reflected sound waves to locate and identify objects)

## EQUIPMENT
Long-toothed snout; large flippers and flukes; small eyes

## WEAKNESS
Can only survive in freshwater

## FACT
River dolphins are born gray and turn pink with age.

## RUBBERNECKER
River dolphins' neck bones are connected by stretchy ligaments, allowing their heads to bend 90 degrees from side to side.

## "HIGH SIX!"
A river dolphin's wide flippers are modified hands. The boto is the only dolphin species with a sixth "finger" bone.

## SAWTOOTH
Botos grasp and chew prey with inflexible jaws that contain up to 70 teeth.

## HALF-TIME
One half of a river dolphin's brain can sleep while the other is awake.

## GEOGRAPHY
Amazonian and Orinoco river systems

## HABITAT
Swishes along rivers and through flooded forests

# RIVER ROVER

Pink-skinned botos, or Amazon river dolphins, won't win any beauty contests, but these creatures could capture top prizes for hunting. Botos comb open waters and flooded forests for fish, their agile movements helping them catch prey. This flexibility also aids in defense: when evading capture, they turn and twist quickly and crazily, making them difficult to track.

**ENEMY**

### HUMANS
Although they share space with hunters as fierce as anacondas and jaguars, botos are killed most often when snared in fishing nets.

**PREY**

### PIRANHAS
Amazon river dolphins rule rainforest waters. They enjoy more than 50 species of fish, including dangerous and sharp-toothed piranhas.

### TURTLES
Botos are adept at navigating flooded forest floors. They hunt turtles in areas other river animals can't reach.

### CRABS
In murky waters, river dolphins locate hiding crabs by emitting sounds that bounce back and reveal the crabs' locations.

## BOTO
*Inia geoffrensis*

LENGTH: **6 FEET (2 M)**   WEIGHT: **275 POUNDS (125 KG)**

**INTELLIGENCE**
■■■■■■■■□□

**AGILITY**
■■■■■■■■■□

**STRENGTH**
■■■■■□■■■■□

**ENDURANCE**
■■■■■■■□■□

**SPEED**
■■■■■■■□■□

**ATTACK**
■■■■□■■□■□

# RAINFOREST CHALLENGE

From the storm-swept canopy, down the armored trunks of the midstory, to the disease-filled understory and flooded forest floor, a gauntlet of challenges awaits rainforest inhabitants at every level. In this extreme environment, staying alive takes special skills—and survival is not a game.

## RAINFOREST LEVELS

EMERGENT LAYER

CANOPY

MIDSTORY

UNDERSTORY

FLOOR

### SHADOWLANDS
Most animals live in the canopy, where food and light are plentiful. As little as 1 percent of available sunlight filters through the canopy, midstory, and understory to the barren forest floor. Down in the dark, decomposers, such as fungi, insects, and bacteria, survive in the deep leaf layer.

**STRANGLER FIGS**

**PITCHER PLANTS**

## TERRIFYING TREES

Many hungry plant species have developed alternative energy plans and treacherous defenses. Strangler figs wrap around other trees and live off them like parasites. Pitcher plants trap and eat insects. Still other plants grow spikes and thorns to keep invaders at bay.

**LUNGFISH**

## HIGH WATERS

Amazon waters reportedly flood as high as 40 feet (12 m) in the wet season and send animals into the trees. In the dry season, waters recede, stranding fish in isolated ponds. Lungfish breathe air and move from pool to shrinking pool to survive.

## MUD HOLES

High water content and slow drainage can turn regular soil into dangerous quicksand. This smothering mud can engulf any creature unlucky enough to venture onto its surface.

**BANYAN TREES**

## STORM WARNING

Tropical cyclones whip through Australasian rainforests. Violent storms can knock out up to one-third of a forest's trees. Banyan trees grow buttresses (reinforcing trunks) for stability. Even so, winds up to 125 miles per hour (200 kph) wipe out bats, birds, and other canopy dwellers.

## GERM FACTORY

Warm, humid rainforest temperatures create perfect breeding grounds for insects, bacteria, fungi, and other disease-causing organisms. Dark-colored animals, such as black leopards and jaguars, are more common in rainforests because the same trait that makes fur black may also provide better defenses against viruses.

**BLACK JAGUARS**

# GLOSSARY

**algae** Plantlike organisms that grow in water or damp conditions. Green algae grows in the fur of sloths and provides camouflage.

**ally** An animal that helps another animal, usually to the mutual benefit of both.

**Amazon** The Amazon River stretches about 4,000 miles (6,437 km) long. It flows from the Peruvian Andes to the Atlantic Ocean in northern Brazil. The Amazon basin is the area drained by the Amazon River. It stretches from northern Brazil into Venezuela, Colombia, Ecuador, Peru, and Bolivia and is home to the largest rainforest in the world.

**amphibian** A cold-blooded animal that lives in the water as a larvae, but on land as an adult.

**antenna** One of a pair of slender, movable, and segmented sensory organs on the head of an arthropod. Arthropods, such as insects or crabs, use their antennae to sense movement, temperature, smells, or even tastes.

**aquatic** Growing or living in freshwater or saltwater. Aquatic animals live in water for most or all of their lives.

**biodiversity** The variety of living organisms in an environment, as indicated by numbers of different species of plants and animals. Rainforests are the most biologically diverse environments in the world.

**bromeliad** One of a family of flowering plants that is able to store water in cups formed by tightly overlapping leaf bases. Pools of water that form in bromeliads make ideal nursery ponds for developing tadpoles.

**buoyant** Capable of floating easily in water.

**camouflage** A physical characteristic that helps an animal blend into its environment to hide from predators.

**canine teeth** The two pairs of pointed teeth on the top and bottom of the mouth. Most meat eaters have long, sharp canines that help them tear flesh.

**canopy** The primary layer of the rainforest made up of the crowns of trees. Leaves and branches intersect to catch most of the sunlight and form a roof over the layers below. The canopy is home to many animals, including monkeys, snakes, birds, and frogs.

**counterbalance** A weight that balances another. A basilisk lizard's tail balances the weight of its body so that the lizard doesn't tip over when running.

**deciduous** Deciduous forests are made up of plants that shed their leaves and become dormant during cold seasons. Most rainforests are not considered deciduous. They are made up of broad-leaf trees that grow continuously.

**draculin** A substance found in vampire bat saliva that prevents blood from clotting. Draculin is stronger than any other known blood thinner. Its derivative, DSPA, is in medications prescribed for both heart attack and stroke patients.

**drag** In physics, something that slows down motion. Drag is produced by moving against air or water. Sugar gliders are slowed by drag when jumping through the air between trees.

**echolocation** A process for navigating or sensing the location of objects (such as prey) by reflecting sound waves. Dolphins emit clicking sounds that bounce off solid forms and then echo back, telling them the location, size, and shape of unseen objects.

**emergent layer** The topmost layer of the rainforest made up of widely spaced trees that extend above the canopy.

**enemy** An animal that is harmful or has a negative relationship with another animal.

**fang** One of a pair of long, sharp teeth used by animals to grasp, seize, or tear. Many snakes have fangs that are hollow and poison filled.

**fluke** The back "fin" on a dolphin or whale tail. Boto flukes are oddly large. Flukes are moved up and down to propel the animals through the water and act as a rudder, or stabilizer.

**forest floor** The bottommost layer of the rainforest. It receives very little sunlight and contains plants adapted to low light as well as decaying plant and animal matter. It is home to many insects, reptiles, and a few mammals that do not dwell in trees.

**Guianas** A region of South America including Suriname, Guyana, and French Guiana.

**habitat** The environment where an animal is best suited to live in the wild.

**hibernate** To pass the winter in a sleeping or resting state. Hibernating animals conserve energy by lowering their temperatures and breathing, metabolic, and heart rates.

**infrared** Light or energy waves that are beyond the spectrum visible to humans on the red end. Infrared waves are often experienced as heat. Emerald green boas have sensory organs near their mouths that detect the heat waves and help them locate predators or prey.

**ligament**  A tough band of flexible tissue that connects bones or holds organs in place.

**mangrove**  An area of dense trees or shrubs that grow in salty marshes or shallow saltwater, such as flooded rainforests.

**marsupial**  An order of mammals, including opossums, wombats, and kangaroos, that have pouches to carry their young. Sugar gliders have pouches that carry their young and protect them from impact when they land.

**melanin**  A class of pigments found in all forms of animal life that cause the dark color of skin, hair, scales, and more.

**metabolism**  The process in living organisms whereby energy is built up and stored, or food is broken down and transformed into the energy that the organism needs to move, eat, and otherwise function.

**midstory**  The middle layer of the rainforest between the canopy and the understory. The midstory consists of midsize trees and shrubs. It is not as sunny as the canopy.

**molting**  The periodic shedding of a creature's outer layer. The cast-off shell or skin is replaced by new growth. Spiders such as the Brazilian salmon pink bird eater molt many times throughout their lives.

**omnivore**  An animal that eats both plant and animal food sources.

**Orinoco**  The Orinoco River is one of the largest rivers in South America. It flows through most of Venezuela, part of Colombia, a small portion of the Guianas, and then empties into the Atlantic Ocean. The Orinoco basin extends from the Andes mountain range to the edge of the Guianas.

**Paraná-Paraguay**  The second-largest river system in South America, the Paraná-Paraguay flows through Argentina, Paraguay, and Brazil.

**patagium**  The fold of skin, or membrane, extending from the body and connecting the front and back limbs of bats and gliding mammals, such as sugar gliders.

**predator**  An animal that hunts other animals for the food it needs to survive.

**prehensile**  A physical trait that is adapted for holding or grasping. For instance, animals like tamanduas and snakes have tails that wrap around branches to hold them in place.

**prey**  Animals that are hunted and eaten by other animals.

**rainforest**  A region with dense tree coverage that receives over 8 feet (2.5 m) of rain a year. Home to more than half of the animal species living on Earth, rainforests once covered 14 percent of the world's surface but now cover 6 percent.

**savanna**  A region with tropical or subtropical weather, wide grasslands, and scattered trees.

**scrubland**  An area characterized by the presence of shrubs, grasses, and herbs.

**shoal**  A school or group of fish. Piranhas cluster in shoals of ten to one hundred fish.

**siphon**  A tube that draws liquid.

**sonic**  Anything that relates to, produces, or uses sound waves. Lines of muscle on the sides of piranhas pick up sonic vibrations, allowing them to "hear" approaching fish.

**subtropical**  The geographical regions that border the tropical zone between 20 and 40 degrees in both latitudes. Subtropical regions have warm winters and hot summers.

**termite**  A soft-bodied insect that lives in colonies and feeds on wood. Termites eat mostly dead wood in rainforests.

**territory**  An area that is occupied and defended by an animal or group of animals. Jaguar males do not like to share territory with other males but will share with females.

**tropical**  The geographical region between the two parallel latitudes that lie 23.5 degrees north and south of the equator. Tropical rainforests are found in Asia, Australia, Africa, South America, Central America, Mexico, and on the Pacific Islands. Average temperatures in the tropical rainforests are higher than 76°F (26°C) most of the year.

**understory**  The layer of the rainforest between the midstory and the forest floor. The understory is characterized by shorter trees such as palms and young saplings. Birds and reptiles live at this level along with predators such as constrictors and jaguars.

**venom**  A poisonous substance produced by snakes, spiders, and other insects that can be injected by biting or stinging into the tissue of prey to paralyze or kill.

**CREDITS**

All illustrations by **Liberum Donum** (Juan Calle, Santiago Calle, Andres Penagos).

All images courtesy of **Shutterstock** unless noted below.
**Age Fotostock:** 22 bottom
**Alamy:** 10 main; 23 main; 45 far bottom right
**Corbis:** 31 main
**Getty:** front cover; 20 main
**iStock:** 27 main; 34 main; 44 far top right; 45 far top left; 45 (unfolded) far left and far right
**Minden Pictures:** 24 main (Thomas Marent); 38 main (Scott Linstead); 40 bottom (Pete Oxford); 41 main (Tui De Roy); 42 main (Kevin Schafer)
**National Geographic Image Collection:** 14 main (Roy Toft); 37 main (Claus Meyer)
**Photolibrary:** 9 main (Joe McDonald)
**Science Photo Library:** 18 bottom (Stan Wayman/ Photo Researchers, Inc.)

**ACKNOWLEDGMENTS**

Special thanks to Jacqueline Aaron, Karen Clarke, Bret Hansen, Sheila Masson, Susan McCombs, and Marisa Solís.